# The Youth We Left Behind

Ankita Dhal

BookLeaf Publishing

India | USA | UK

Presentation by *BookLeaf Publishing*

Web: www.bookleafpub.com

E-mail: info@bookleafpub.com

ISBN: 9789363313347

First edition 2024

*To all those who have loved and lost.*

*Especially my mother.*

# ACKNOWLEDGEMENT

I share my gratitude with all the people who have so beautifully and fiercely stood by me in times of hardship and when grief seemed to be swallowing me whole. To my family, my mother who is the central core of my very being and the loss of whom is the biggest tragedy of my life. My father who is growing into himself and his role for us and has always been an inspiration for striving to be my best self. My sister, Amrita Dhal who taught me everything I know and more, who is my biggest cheerleader and my biggest critic - as sisters should be.

My closest confidants and companions Bhavi Jagatia and Ali Azmi. Bhavi was the first friend I ever chose on my own and to that day we met in kindergarten, I will be forever grateful. To Ali Azmi, who has inspired so much of my love and creativity, who teaches me to be kind and patient.

To Aamir Qazi, my first companion in poetry and in dreaming for a better future. And to many more friends who have shown me what the beauty of life is all about, who are deeply introspective and unique, and make every moment on this planet worth suffering and laughing through - Pooja, Aarish, Nirmohi, Swaraj, Saniya, Megha, Krupa, Saloni and my Busride friends. To those who have left and some who have made their way back through the winter of youth.

Thank you for your support and encouragement.

# PREFACE

In writing 'The Youth We Left Behind' I sought to explore the profound and often unspoken sorrows that linger in the cold seasons of our lives as we step into adulthood. This collection stems from personal reflections and the universal experience of loss and longing, for family, for love and for community. It is a rich collection of deeply intimate stories from my youth as I archive them almost like a secret diary. Themes of grief, loss, and the passage of time are prominently featured throughout this work. These writings cover various topics, including boredom, existentialism, anxiety, depression, and the struggle for meaning in everyday life while coping with grief and c-ptsd.

Through these poems, I aim to create a space where readers can find solace and a sense of shared understanding. Whether your grief comes from losing a loved one, a friend or a lover, or most

importantly the grief of losing yourself
- I hope you find a home in these
words.

# Cities

Can you remember people
Like you remember cities?
And can cities be made of just a few
people?
Can some people seem like the
memory of an entire city?
If yes, then this City feels like a ghost
town of people that used to live here
With me, and now - it's just, mostly me
I wonder if I'm somebody's ghost-town
too, will you think of me when you
think of Bombay?
The brine, the sea, the sunsets, the
sunrise - the dull cloudy days and the
humid sun

The smell of smoke mixed with a
melting pot of masalas and
multiculturalism
Art and graffiti alike on the walls and
the shop fronts
The forever under construction city
Trying to improve but not really
making any visible progress
The stop and speed limit signs shining
in yellow against the black-holes of
pot-holes
Tell me, do you think of me when you
see the unreachable tall palm trees? Or
the keystones of beautiful women on
the colonial buildings?
Because I think of all of you, in every
crevice of this gigantic city - it's all just
you.

# A Time Called You

Do you think we can time travel?
I think we already are
We are trapped in the past
Searching for the future
Never fully here or there
Pulled towards every possibility
but the now
Maybe we don't have to invent it
Because  we've been doing it forever
How else do you explain this de ja vu of
memories that have never happened,
not just yet?
You're not the answer I was looking for
Neither am I that, for you
Are we the question then ?
Give me a sign,
You'll see it when you want to

Signs exist only when
you seek them out
So tell me, you reading this, is it a sign?
Did I give you one or did you give me
mine?

# Notes on Grief

I saw the ember's rise from your
burning body,
Then why do I keep hoping for a text
message from you every dusk?
"Bahariluniki?" (Have you left?)
I saw the blues and blacks on your skin,
I wailed at you and heard nothing back
Yet I continue to call out for you in my
head all the time
Hoping that your voice will echo back
an answer
Where did your voice go?
Where did you go?
I felt the icy touch of your wrists and
carried you in my arms
Then why do I still feel like you're just
on a long due vacation

and one of these days, against all
forensic evidence
I'll unlock the door to find you sitting
right there,
But this time you'll be smiling instead
of that sea of blankness that slid across
your face

Some moments are starting to have a
strange quietness in my head,
in my heart.
The energy inside that used to seem
like a possible soul, seems missing
my exterior feels like a cracked glass,
not leaking just yet
and the water inside is so incredibly
still, that sometimes it feels like it's an
empty vessel
It feels wrong, sinful and ignorant to
move forward,
But the world continued
to rotate and revolve.
People went on with their lives,
some fell in love, some fought,
Some revolutions grew
and some fused.
Some packed up and left, while some
returned back home.

It's been 20 days now,
and the sun still rises
but how can I, without you.

# Finalities

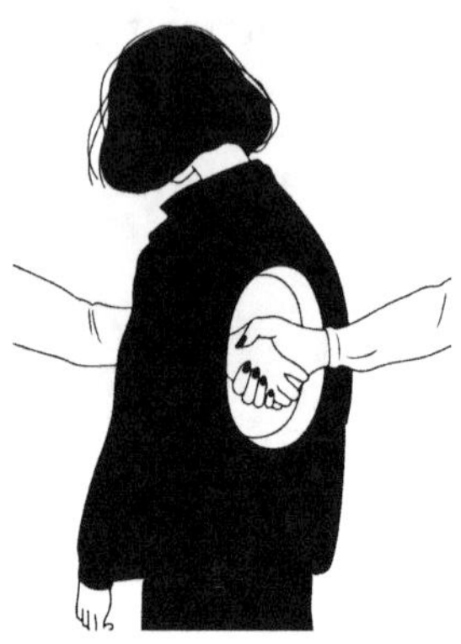

I'm losing you between moments of
remembering our life and,
the last moments I spent with you
after you passed
Images of both come and go, each
causing specific feelings of loss
that are unique each time I feel them
The image of you lifeless on the couch,
causes a physical pain in my heart
making it go beating
at different speeds
as waves of anxiety pass
through my body
I struggle to remember and cloud that
horrific moment
with memories of the past,

that are otherwise so accessible
They just seem to vanish at will

I had no idea a single small little brain
could repress this much horror and
beauty together.
These boxes keep opening
on their own.
And the one person I want to tell them
about, is you.
The finality of death surrounds me
more and more each day.
How is a person here one minute,
and not there the other?
How has this become my life?
There's a hollowness here
Somedays I sit with it trying to find
something in it
A magical fullness that's been missing
since you died
And some days as I search
I uncover an immensity of pain
Suddenly spilling out like boiling tea
Its fluidity surrounds me
Takes over, hurting me so wholly that
for a moment I mistake it for fullness
again.

# 

If dreaming is free
Then why are dreams so expensive  ?
/
Khud mein sab rakhne ki aadat si ho
gayi hai
Khamoshi mein Jeene ki aadat si ho
gayi hai
Kash tumhe apni peheliya batayi hoti
Shayad aaj akelepan mein suljhane ki
aadat na hoti
Iss roz ke jeene se thakaan si hogayi
hai.
/
If my life isn't being witnessed
anymore
Does it mean I have ceased to exist?

If I didn't post about it
Did it even happen?
/
Khud mein hi uljeh rahoge, toh iss
duniya ko kab suljhaogey?
/
Time feels like a circle now
It goes on and on
I feel dragged along with it
As though I don't remember what
control felt like
I keep expecting to stop moving in
these circles
Or atleast pause and step out of line
for a second, catch a breath
But why can't I?

# Remember me?

Why do I remember all the lovers who
never quite loved me right
Why has this compounded grief
untangled all the times
that I lost the one?
Where had your skeletons been
hiding? Deep in the dark corners of my
subconscious
Seems as though my mother died with
the shield that protects my heart and
my mind, all the memories are
bleeding out now.
The first love and how
he ruined my self esteem,
But with it I remember the nights he
said he dreamt of me, the mountains
we would climb and the how we would

fall asleep under the constellations we
pretended to know all about
The second, that stole some more of
my firsts, the one that made me wait
longer than I needed to,
but with it I remember the countless
calls and the limited walks, our hands
intertwined, an anticipation that made
my heart beat so fast
I thought I would die.
The one in-between, who made the
simple realm of friendship
questionable, but with it I remember
how safe I felt, how loved,
how important.
I yearn for that warmth now that I
seemed to have faded in his mind.
And lastly the one who broke my heart,
my mind, my resolve
and everything in between into more
pieces than I could quantify.
His love was always there at his own
convenience,
but never really there for mine.
Yet, I remember your laugh and the
way your eyes glistened, and I hate
that I remember them. When I saw
you smile on that Christmas night,

it was a bad addiction wasn't it,
him and I?
Why are your skeletons sliding out of
this closet now?
Maybe the grief has made the locks so
weak, they can't hold you in any longer.
It's painful enough to long for
someone I truly cherish and care for, I
can't keep up with longing for broken
bones too.
What is left to offer to ghosts for them
to leave me alone in this graveyard of
memories?
How do I reconcile with your
memories? When I think of young love,
a coming of age initiation
It wasn't love until it felt like the whole
world had stopped spinning.
A heartbreak meant that the world
suddenly began spinning again, only
this time - at a hundred spins per
second. Shifting the ground beneath
your feet, leaving you out of sight and
dizzy, making you fall apart in every
perceivable way.
As the youth leaves my years, I'm
slowly realizing that falling in love

can feel in tune with the rest of the
world too
And when it breaks, it can happen in
cordial glances and praises.
It can acknowledge the pain of
separation and handle honest heavy
hearted goodbyes. It can exist in your
deep subconscious as a gentle gray
memory, instead of holding a dark
dungeon like air.
It can grieve together. I wish I could go
back to all of my past lives, to all the
people that I left behind and the ones
that left me.
To have one last honest conversation.
I wish we could look each other in the
eye and take a pause while the world
spun around - To say, it changed me, it
gave me joy and it gave me pain and it
haunts who I will become.
But for now,
Take care, I will remember you.

# Fragile

Sometimes I feel like
If someone stared into my eyes long
and hard enough
longer than a minute, perhaps
I would shatter into a million pieces
Like a fragile cracked ceramic plate
Pushed to persevere
in the china cabinet,
when it's clearly run out
of its glory days
and meant to retire
only to shatter by an achingly long
overdue glance
I work relentlessly, endlessly
Maybe so I don't have to think

or feel a thing
I go on like a machine
And I break like a machine
Trying to self - repair
over and over again
I'm exhausted now, I think I've worn
out, become outdated
Sometimes I think it might be best to
turn the power off
Switch off the lights
Turn down the sounds and voices
And see, If I could still breathe without
the electricity and the oxygen

# All I Wanted Was to Swim

It's been a while,
that I've found the storms attractive
Whether it was the rain,
Or the thunderstorms
Whether it was in your heart or mine,
It's been a while that I've tried to chase
those tornados
The terrible kind
Swirling above seas with all the
monsters
Screaming with their tails captured in
the swirls
It's been some time
that I've wanted to feel
the thrashing of the waves
Against my skin

The salt filling my lungs
Trying to float against the buoyancy
It's been a few or more now
That I've purposely drowned in the sea
To watch the sunlight seep in through
the waves, and maybe through your
eyes

# Past Lives

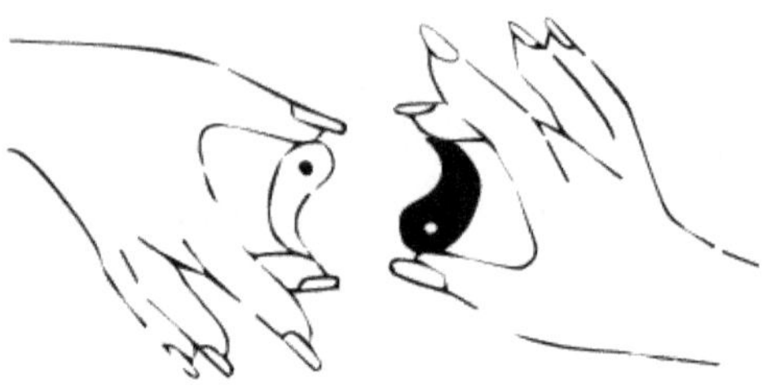

Have you enjoyed growing up? you ask
I always wondered about you
At some point who we used to be and
everything we lived through together
became memories,
A past life
When I think of the age of 14,
I think of you
When I crave my sharp aggressive
teenage authenticity, I think of you
When I recall that first heartbreak, the
first misunderstood circumstance,
I think of us
A decade has passed since we walked
out those halls
With stolen glances, smiles,
silent walks, secret notes
and late night text messages

The first act of rebellion in our
conservative brown homes
The dreams and ambitions we spoke of
everyday, the false promises of seeing
it all play out with each other
The smell of fresh juice being churned
at the restaurant
we stood in front of after-school,
While we argued and talked through
every last minute, before our parents
could notice us waste our future away
The birthday cards, the rings, the
chance encounter at the local book
store, the hours we spent loving Potter
I still remember each time I rolled my
eyes at your arrogance when I didn't
care for it
I still remember the first time we
smiled at each other in the
examination hall and how my stomach
turned upside down
Both of us, walking in late, scramming
to find a spot for our bags and then
rushing to our seats - you at the front
row and I at the back - a metaphor for
what was to come
Something made me want to look at
you again, and so were you

Time felt like it stood still and I
involuntarily smiled at you for the very
first time only to do it a million times
over
How that smile turned the axis of my
little teenage life off center for a while
The mind games, the hesitation, the
proclamations, the courage
The late night dreams discussed like
our little secret, the Christmas dances,
the breaktime rendezvous
The plays we wrote, the intercom calls
we made the first chance we left the
city far away from the rules of our
families,
The farewells we hosted. Ahh the irony,
that we never got a farewell of our own
I still remember the first time your
arrogance affected my self worth
I still remember the last time we didn't
steal any glances and walked away
without any secret smiles
I still remember the abandonment and
grief as if it all happened just yesterday,
when you pulled away overnight
I still remember checking my phone
waiting to understand what went
wrong

What had I done wrong? Was I not
enough? Did I screw up?
I'm not 14 anymore, but I carry that
wounded 14 year old girl with me
wherever I go
Sometimes I hate it and sometimes I
wanna turn back time and be her
With her heavy heart I also carry the
girl who was as warm as the sun and
drawn to your rain
It's strange how grief opens up a
Pandora's box
Was I meant to meet you again? Is that
why my dreams were haunted for the
past few years?
What would we look like had we
stayed in touch?
In another universe did it play out
differently?
We're softer now,  we're carrying a lot
more pain now
We were naive then, arrogant, angry
and so easily careless
When beneath all of those
performative layers, existed a deep
attachment and care
We're past 25 now - so brutally self
aware

Have you enjoyed growing up?
Does it matter because we're still
growing up aren't we?
As we sit here together, a decade later
Why does it feel like I'm feeling all of
this for the very first time?
as if we're cheating time
or is time cheating us?
I thought memories don't change
you said memories meant pain for you
I wish meeting again at 25  and
traveling back in time for the night,
changed that for you
I wish the fog of pain cast over our past
lives can dissipate,
like the clouds clearing in the morning
as the sun rises
I wish as the fog dissipates, we
remember the mountains and
constellations as much as we
remember the rain
memories can change, they can evolve
like we have, So far from 14 and yet so
close

# Dipti Allay

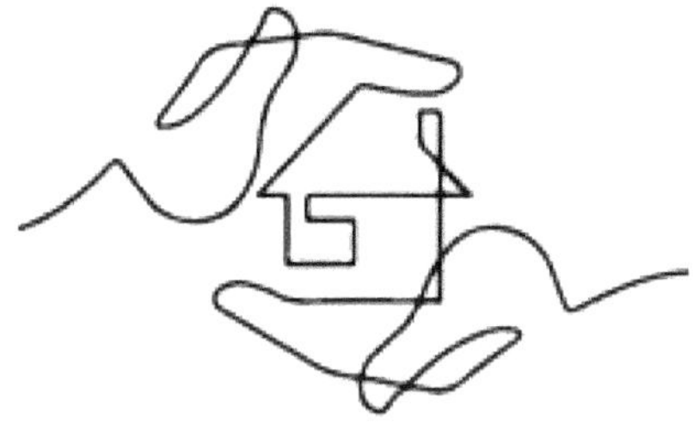

I have a physical reaction every time I
hear the bells ring
in our neighbors house,
they ring when the clock turns 7pm as
the dusk sets in and it feels almost as if
the ghost of you just passed through
my body
ringing the same bells in my cells.
The bells, delicately carried in your left
hand and concentrating on bringing
good energy into the house for your
daughters and husband through the
flame in your right hand,
a plea to god every single day - to
protect, to keep healthy, to bring joy
and courage, to help your family thrive
the brass diya glistened with your ghee
fingerprints as the flame burnt

through the night - carrying all your
hopes and desires
none for yourself and thousands for
everyone else.
And now we sit here, listening
vicariously to the sound of someone
else's bells that no longer ring here -
in the home built without you, one
with no physical traces of you
but your absence echoes in every
presence of you that percolates
through all our
handpicked colors and items
We decorate this house as a museum
of your memory, reluctantly collecting
new ones in our hearts - plastering the
walls with your frozen smiles in
photographs so desperate to tell the
visitor about you who lived, who lives
here - somewhere, somehow, invisible,
omnipresent, forever gone.
We named this house after you, Dipti
Aalay. We made a marble mandir for
you and set up all your idols with care,
just as you would've. Are we praying to
you or to them?

Papa lights the Diya every day as dusk
sets in, but there are no ringing bell
sounds.
The brass numbers - 1302 Dhal's
glistens underneath your name that is
apparently our home - unsettled with
some glossy Araldite
to build a home by the cinematic
orchestra playing coincidently (?) as I
unwrap the letters and I weep - for
your name will be the only home that
we search for, for the rest of our lives.

# The Youth of My Youth

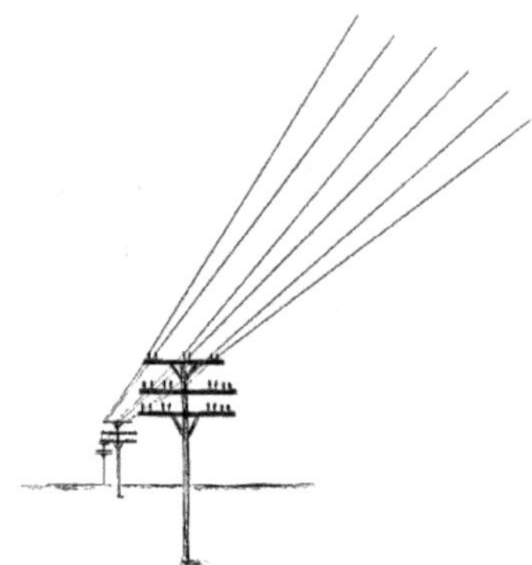

These streets
They're so familiar
The memories of my first first love
lingers in the traffic signal that has
been here forever
It rings through the hawkers calls
It shines and glimmers over the bright
signs and boards of the shops we
stood by.
These streets are so irrelevant to the
city
Just a blip on the map
But they make the city of me
They've helped build it up
I'm still delayering and un-mapping
these streets
I still don't understand them,

Even though they feel ancient and
frozen in time
The people that made all my firsts are
gone
But these alleys remain
And I stumble upon them
unexpectedly at every other turn
Not knowing what to think or do
Other than flashing a knowing smile
At the ghost of myself living through
that time.

# We're just Friends

This line that we walk on
the thin, fragile, silky line
with its threads slightly disintegrating,
There was a time when it was not
complicated,
there was a time
when You and I
could just sleep in the field
singing chasing cars,
and not feel this way
some days I forget that a time like that
existed, platonic, defined, separate
some days I look at you and forget
that the only kind of feelings
I should have for you

are of purity and affection
of gratitude and unmarred perfection
It's so easy to confuse comfort with
love these days.
Some days I get a little caught up in
the way you talk
and the stories you tell, pausing and
drifting every other minute
I smile a little more than I should as I
watch you digress
Even if I've heard them all the same
Some days I catch a glimpse of you
when you're not looking
And I slip a wow
Somedays I doubt if that was just
affection or lust?
what would it be like, if we were the
only ones walking this street
What would it be like if you were
thinking this too?
Oh this line, that we try to walk on, run
away from,
It used to smoother, thicker, stronger,
with lesser threads coming off
It was easier to brush it off when I
didn't understand you
But it's been years now,
the line has worn off,

i know you like a habit
that's hard not to love
the thought of a You and I should
repulse me as it did long ago
but this is what growing up does, all
your imperfections only make you
more human
it was easier to categorize it as the
trivial friend-zone
or an ever important friendship on the
others
that I simply could not afford to crack
When did the definitions become
irrelevant?
When did controlling myself from
staring into your eyes get so difficult?
it's not everyday that I want to write a
poem of unrequited love for you
some days it's just blissful friendship
then what is it? if not everyday
If not the maddening great love that
haunts literature, then what are we?
the in-between awkward but heartfelt
exchanges
of 'I miss you and I love you's'
what would I do without -
"I'll be there for you'

why do I remember them when i'm
trying so hard to drown in love with
someone else,
why has your friendship become,
the ultimate goal of an ideal love that I
search for in the faces around us
yet stop at yours for an extra
millisecond that only I and my
skipping heartbeat can detect
Why do I get breathless when you look
at someone else like that?
when it's clear we should be on the
other side of the line,
but if it is, then why does my mind feel
so foggy, when that dim light hits your
face and the smoke from your
cigarette fades across your mouth
And for a second the alluring
intoxication of both becomes one in
the same
Why do I forget the limits, the
boundaries?
but I don't cross the line, I only stumble
upon it
that is what consumes me at night as
we say our goodbyes
I watch over your back as you walk
away

Would it be better to fall off the line or
to take a step back?
I love the theory of parallel universes
for it
validates the existence of  a you and I,
but I'm tired of throwing all my dreams
into these other realms
hoping a version of me lived the life I
crave for on the  some-days;
the inability to pick a side in my own
universe
for I know I hate convention and social
constructs
But it's driving me crazy to not have
one for you
I try not to get used to you, when it
gets bad.
I try to not waste all my time with you.
I try not to rely on your warmth,
some days to avoid falling for you, and
some days to avoid confusing
the white horses you ride on
Maybe you're just meant to save me
and I'm meant to save you
One more string, One more time and
we could break for good.
Yet, knowing this why do I want to risk
it all when -

I should be lying down in the field
singing chasing cars as only 'friends'

# Destiny

I've already typed the text message
That declares the end of us
Yet, somehow after all the
disappointments
I still can't seem to send it off
What is it about us that's so difficult to
let go?
We sung about destiny in our golden
years
That destiny is haunting me now
It keeps me stuck in the past, stuck
with you
When you've not stuck with me
It's been 8 years since that fateful
morning

When I gathered the courage to speak
to you
I wonder, will we still be stuck in this
destiny 8 years later?
Will we ever change?
When you said to me all those years
ago,
That we could be alone together
forever,
I didn't think I'd end up feeling so
alone in this, even with you by my side.
When did our destiny become so
tragic?

# Blue Midnights

Didn't think I would stand here
Never believed I would enjoy this
some nights feel good only with the
old friends
but these days strangers make me
laugh too
sitting in the rickshaw
streetlights becoming glowing lines
the sound of laughter staying longer in
my ears
when the walls that are mundane
make me smile at 1am.
Trying so hard to not stutter and fall
we convince each other, we're fine
as we walk into a room full of lights
our faces turn blue and red in the
night

the roaring voices fill up our empty
hearts
and for a minute I swear I can feel my
soul still and present
shaking hands and feet, vibrating
floors
I've never met you but I like you
and I'll never remember you again
when I wake up from this dream
stay here still staring at me,
we're young and we're wrong
that's what makes this okay
we bash and scream at each other,
today our differences and moralities
really don't matter
I stand here in the middle, breathing it
all in
before it all falls apart
there's a warmth in my veins,
this is the only moment I always
remember
for a second its black and when it
lights up again
I see my friends laughing, living and
unburdened
wasting our youth away
its past midnight and I never thought I
would enjoy being awake this way

I don't know what I've had
but I will in the morning
when we wake up in a mess
I'll still want that blue midnight all over
again

# The Balcony

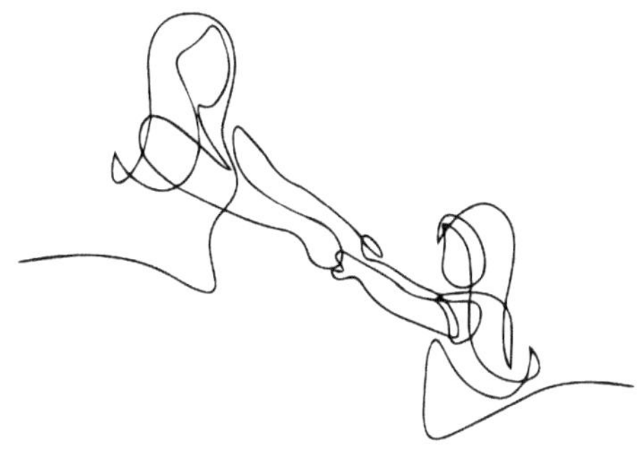

I've been thinking of writing. But
where do I begin?
I'm afraid, with mum, old friends and
the future, I've lost my words too
Is it an obligation? Is it evidence, is it
witnessing or is it the validation ?
What do I seek with these words
anymore?
I've been quietly walking in my mind
now, trying to figure it all out
Walking by the streets, how they exist
here and there
How you used to exist in them, here
and there
Today I stood in front of the apartment,
that was once ours
The only balcony I ever loved,

I saw a woman standing in the one
below, watching as you once did, long
ago
Spying on the men hovering around
your daughter, spying on your
daughter's hearts
We saw summers pass by, sat on the
cold terrazzo on winter nights
watching the dusty sky
We saw floods go by, children waving
at us in tragedy
We ran to the terrace when I'd spot the
first kite on Makar Sankranti,
or the first rain hitting the ledge and
our good old cactus plant
Remember how you'd show everyone
when it bloomed once in 13 years?
As the woman stood there, her partner
came out, pushing the four doors
open, calling her in
As they talked and their family's
shadows danced in silhouettes, I saw
us too
I wondered, if I was there right now,
would I tell myself what fate our family
would have?
Would I tell myself you'd die so young?
And stay dead for the rest of my life?

I didn't know the answer, I just stood
there in the dark dim street lights, with
echoes of rickshaw drivers and
passer-bys laughing heartily
I just stood there and watched us, our
old house, our old life, our full life
The trees swayed in soft breeze, the
leaves casting shadows against the
orange hued concrete
Time passed, time was here and going
But I stayed put in the past, holding a
bag of  bananas and dahi that you
should've bought for me
I still see you sometimes, I still hear you
sometimes. Most days I can't tell if it
really is you or if I'm just yearning?
I've declared my birthday as banned
this year,
you died four days later after all
It feels as though my 22nd with you,
making you eat fancy lasagne at that
Pizza Express was the last happy
memory I'll ever make
To be honest,
I'm just afraid to replace it
I don't want anyone to have that
chance

I need you to hold that memory, hold
those 22 years,
Because it's difficult to see many more,
why'd you have to die so young?
You'll never know who I become
I don't think I can ever grow up now
Just as you're stuck at 53, I'm stuck at
22
What should I do? Am I forgetting
you?
Or am I forgetting myself? Isn't that
the same thing?
Is your death my illness? Or is the grief
my illness?
Is it the love I've lost? Or is it the love I
never spoke of that has become this
sickness?
Are these the wounds of the thoughts I
never shared, the feelings I held in,
the pride and self esteem that I let sink
deep in the sea
that are now tearing
the insides of my body
Making me bleed, making me tired
Oh, I'm so tired, I want it to stop
I have run out of words and the silent
screams have made me lose my voice
I want the world to stop spinning

so that I can stand still without feeling
dizzy again
I feel like I'm in a hamster cage
Stuck running and running and
running
Waiting for someone or something to
magically arrive
And to stop the wheel from turning
over again,
so that I can finally get off
and catch my breath
(I could slow down and get off on my
own, but I don't know how)
How can I just take a leap off the
balcony?
Will I find you one the other side

# Year 4, Day 2540

As I sit here, in this shaky rickshaw
with a mask that hides tears glistening
against the traffic lights
a routine developed carefully and
perfected in the last almost 4 years
( almost I say, since we're still 8 hours
away from your 4 year death
anniversary)
as I sit here listening to a playlist about
growing up,
I think - It would be nice if someone
called right now
In a muffled voice I'd say - hi
You'd say - hey, are you okay?
no no,
you just caught me at a bad time

Should I call back later?
it's nice to hear someones voice right
now,
Reality interjects the people in my
head, gosh how can someone read my
mind? how could they call if they
didn't even know why my heart weighs
heavy tonight ?
Were you thinking the same, as your
heart gave away ?
oh how nice it would be if someone
called me right now, if they could feel
the pain radiate in my chest?
how I would get a chance to ask for
help
I had a feeling all day that day, four
years ago,
yet I didn't call, I wish I had
but I don't think about the maybe that
follows this wishful thinking anymore
maybe that's what the passage of time
means
it doesn't heal, though it reveals
that I could not have read your mind
and called
That you'd still not be here
That you still aren't

# Uncertainty

I remember them asking, when I
couldn't even walk straight
"What are you gonna be when you
grow up?"
As little as I did know about the world
and the people in it,
made me say what my dad did, or my
sister, or the things my teachers talked
about
or the what cartoons led me to believe
Even then, in my memories
I remember uncertainty
They asked again a few years down the
line

my hair had grown, my gait more
fragile
"What are your plans for the future?"
some days I'd shrug
some days I'd say what all my friends
were saying, just to get the
conversation done with
other days I'd sit uncomfortably and
avoid eye contact until the subject of
the question
was indeed someone else
a sigh of relief
I woke up wanting to be someone new
each day, my future an array of
distinct personas
A life made of many lives felt like the
most exciting kind
yet those thoughts were frowned upon
apparently I was supposed to pick only
one
discouraged, my shoulder slumped a
little, although the hope was still
strong in my back.
An unprepared uncertainty
They asked again before I graduated
from high school.
"What next? Have you made up your
mind yet?"

I don't know when it happened but
somewhere in 17 years I'd adopted a
dream.
Some dream
words I'd say to hide my thoughts had
now become my concrete future
I got closer and closer,
pages and sheets scribbled upon
desperately
ambition for numbers accounting for
the transformation of dreams into
reality
The haziness between the two started
getting farther, a thick line separating
them.
A Trance-like uncertainty
A few years had passed
They asked again,
"What are you gonna be?"
I no longer know which is better
to wait in the limbo of waking up
disoriented, laziness and exhaustion
clouding
the concept of time, laying on the bed
staring at a ceiling fan
like all of life's lessons could be learnt
right here in this limbo

Or do I take charge? get on an endless
cycling track of destinations,
pressure on the pedals leaving tracks
of creativity
What cost am I paying for these road
marks?
An anxious uncertainty
They ask again, every week
in classrooms,
in protest walks
on phone screens and in loud screams
on the television sets
"What kind of a person will you be?"
am I a person if all my thoughts are a
reproduction of the same bullshit
someone else already did
Am I a person if I never liked any other
colors than the grays?
Am I a person if I don't confine myself?
A nervous uncertainty
I see it in their eyes
we're not there in time yet, but the
questions are here now.
they will ask soon
"What will you do for those who did for
you ?"
But is there a quantifiable measure for
what I got and what I can give?

for all the nights my father worked
for all the time my mother saved
for all these morals and values that I
carry, a heirloom passed down
inherently
some days desperately trying to
embody them and some days trying to
tear them off my flesh and bones
Before I can figure out who I am
I am thrown off course with the
burdens of them asking
"What will you do for the world? How
will you contribute to society?"
There are nights I wonder, if living with
a void for a mind would have been
better
How do you pick a war to fight, a side
to advocate and a point of view to
support
when you find empathy and confusion
towards every headline
with enough words read and heard,
every cause is worth fighting for
when I couldn't pick a future
when I don't understand my past
when I exist in oblivion in the present
How do I answer anything at all?
I ask myself

"Will you ever get there or just float like
a cloud for the rest of eternity?"
"Get where?" I ask.
silence.
An uncertain uncertainty.

# Walk in to some Bougainvillea

Have you ever wanted to dance in a
field of flowers?
I have been dreaming of a lush warm
coloured scenic beauty, lately
a place where breath and the air feels
like a scent
shooting so fast and so unique
through your system,
that it makes the hair on the back of
your neck stand
the joy I could find in picking baskets
of petals and twigs
carefully touching each,
understanding the pricks and the
pollens

memorizing the mesmerizing patterns
and the perfection of geometry
After years of chasing imperfect,
incomplete adventures
maybe I'm finally driving to the one
that won't leave my senses
But careful there, you wouldn't want to
say that out loud
because once you pick and pick and
pick
these flowers out one by one
each passing day one will die
until, the field left barren, the air like a
void then
oh universe, what dilemma have you
left me in?
you know I'm gonna drive there
anyway

# Notes on Love

The lightning outside my window
Shone out of nowhere
It wasn't particularly good weather
But I wasn't asking for a thunderstorm
either
Still when the first stroke of light
Touched the ground and lit the 4am
city
I couldn't help but feel like
I'd been waiting for this nonetheless
The windows shook, doors flew open,
Unrecognizable new sounds unsettled
me
The trees moved in sync with the wind,
the only evidence was the silhouette

And in all of this madness, as you
calmed me down without even trying
on the other side of the phone
The other side of the country
I realized, you are just like the lightning
Vast, brilliant, making all the darkness
go away
Shining, wavering, breaking apart and
a little scary too
And I'm in love with this unexpected
madness
Felt like I was floating in a wide ocean
with no semblance
With no particular wave in mind
Until I see you sailing a boat, a quarter
mile away
Far but still so close in hindsight
Hope to find more than just droplets in
this wide ocean
If I could find you between the dark
indigo and the gray skies of
nothingness
What else could I ask the cosmos to
realign so that these fragile
Tired limbs and bones
Could lie down inches away from your
warmth
And these tissues and this  body could

Fall apart with you
My chest crumbling, Our heart beats in sync
Healing the fabric of our being
You're starting to complete my sentences
Starting to know what I'd say and think it while I say it
You're getting through me now,
Getting to my head,
Noticing the way it works, what I'm possibly feeling and why
It's like reading a person,
But here it's not a just any person, it's me
No edits no aesthetics, no controlled planned appropriated pleasing versions of me,
But just me, And that makes me very unsettled
In a scary and beautiful way
In this big brilliant world
How do two people make it through
Pass through borders and lives and reach each other
Live through years of heartbreaks and experiences to be just the right mix
For someone to fit right into their life

A golden ratio between you and I
Do people become immortal ?
When you think of them in all the
beautiful places you go to without
them?
When you long for their warm
presence
In the cold dark nights with the
moonlight shining high above
Does your longing from deep within,
leave your soul and float among the
pine trees?
Do you think the absent leave a scratch
on the barks? Visible only to the one
who sent out the longing?
Maybe their memories float in the air
along with the dandelions
Maybe when I drive away, the
moonlight will still remember you,
even though you were never here
Always thought I got my heart broken,
a piece left behind with each one
so one day it'd be strong enough to
fight for the that would last
I left a piece of me with each one that
passed by and left me,

Unknowingly, however, hoping
someday, I'll find them, see them and
remake those pieces all over again
When I felt the emptiness of the
incomplete pieces,
I wrote you down before in different
people,
in conversations I never had, in small
specks of sunlight through thick lush
leaves,
I'd see your  light
Now I finally see you and you're
helping bring back every piece, each
day,
In the hopes of rebuilding something
new together
Sometimes I wish I could chase the
sunset holding your hand forever
Sometimes I wish I could stand at the
airport staring at you as you held my
face and walked away, forever
Sometimes I wish I could sit at the
beach and listen to music with you,
watching the sunrise forever
Sometimes I wanna die, sometimes I
wanna live so desperately
Sometimes pain shines so bright, and
love feels so deep and dark

Sometimes I just wanna eat dinner
with my mom forever, sometimes I feel
stuck between them all, all at once.
Through these times, the heart grows
fonder
And with it so does the fear
To love and to have lost -
Taints the hope for the future
Yet to have loved itself
Is evidence enough that just as pain
pervades forever,
So does love - it persists
It's abundant
And it holds you with all your voids and
wounds
How powerful do you think love is?
The only way to truly know, is to lose it
forever
Grief is the key to unlock the
insurmountable experience of love
To lose, is to love

# Are you a sunset?

I picked up guitars when I was twelve
dropped that act soon
I picked up keys when I was fourteen
dropped that act too
I picked up pens and brushes most
often
That love would come and go
I picked up on words
those only accompany me when I
need them so
I've realized that I was simply not the
person
who could pick and keep
I loved the thrill of finding and learning
but I loved learning all at once, more
a year ago I found you,
for the first time, I picked and held
onto
Commitment felt like a long lost friend

that I intended to meet everyday
it's been a year now
and the forever that felt as thick
as the core of the earth
never felt as thin before
what am I to do with myself
its only I to blame
should I have known this inevitability?
or should I say no?
I look at you and I remember the glow
But sometimes a sunset everyday feels
normal too
What if I outgrew you too?
I'll keep saying no
when we met I believed in destiny
for happiness is easy to credit to
destiny
but it's normalcy that does not fit,
in the grand plan the universe made
for you and I
its youth that brings balance to the
mundane and the thrilling
its you that has shown me both
and the time comes now
when I decide to listen
they said if you get through the tough
times, with the ones you love
it will last forever

So it's time to choose
flight or fight?
passion only lasts a quarter of a
lifetime,
its practice that diligently
holds your hand every day
and so you live to fight another day
pick it up, yourself and them
you are here to stay.
(update: sunsets never feel normal, you
just gotta give it a moment for it to
become magical)

# You still sing your sentences

I sing my sentences
My words seem like thinking about
them might cause them to shatter and
make you bleed
My eyes are expressive like a dark swan
If I was a color I would be a lilac, but
sharper, brighter, with a tinge of pink
or red ?
Tragic how I see melancholy in my
sentences
Like if I said too much, I would shatter
and if said too less my lungs would
collapse into themselves
My eyes feel tired to me, dark and dull
sometimes

I feel limitless and yet empty like the
blues and greens of the sea
Who is this you see? Is it really me?
Or had I forgotten what I looked like?
I must not value myself, these days I've
been dreaming of vanishing away
I must not value myself, because I feel
strangely assured that I will not be
missed
Lately all I see are ghosts, everywhere I
go, places, restaurants, markets
I feel stuck in the past
Lately all I see is ghosts
Unable to feel the life in anything
Nightmares haunt my daydreams, and
the days passing by feel like
nightmares
You said I write in circles,
What do I do, I'm so tired of trying to
do it all
I would rather be trapped in 360
Than reconcile with the others
when the other is me and I am the
other? do I really know that I am better
than I think I am
or are both beings  just brilliant
performances?

are we ever good enough - a question
so large and yet so simple
and it gnaws at my skin so deeply that
the blood doesn't seem enough
lately - I feel despicable,
like I am playing charades
I am a Phoenix unable to be reborn
stuck in the ashes
oh so gray that was once golden
like the stardust in my eyes and my
veins
molten and rotten
desperate to be set free
caged by my own inhibitions
betrayed by the mind that knows it
can do better that it can be better
I feel breathless lately - craving
reconciliation
dreaming of a far away land
And reuniting with the Albatross
the desire is eating me alive
and so I scrape through the ashes
Gnawing, waiting, for it to pass
waiting to fly again, I work relentlessly,
endlessly
Maybe so I don't have to think or feel a
thing

I do sing my sentences, but
somewhere down the line
I forgot the tune
The embrace in your eyes
Felt like a memory of a hug we never
had
I used to be a song and then I let
myself remain trapped in a nostalgic
melody
I'm ready now, to become the
conductor of this orchestra
If I must perform anyway, let's do it for
the audience, that is me